THE
SALEM
WITCHCRAFT
TRIALS

THE
SALEM
WITCHCRAFT
TRIALS

KAREN ZEINERT

CONTRA COSTA COUNTY LIBRARY
Franklin Watts
New York / London / Toronto / Sydney
A Venture Book

Frontis: accusation of a "bedeviled"
girl during a Salem witchcraft trial

Library of Congress Cataloging-in-Publication Data

Zeinert, Karen.
The Salem witchcraft trials / by Karen Zeinert.
p.   cm.—(A Venture book)
Bibliography: p.
Includes index.
Summary: Relates the causes, events, and aftermath of the
witchcraft trials which took place in Salem, Massachusetts, in
the early 1690's and resulted in the deaths of more than
nineteen people.
ISBN 0-521-10673-X
1. Trials (Witchcraft)—Massachusetts—Salem—Juvenile
literature. 2. Salem (Mass.)—History—Juvenile literature.
[I. Trials (Witchcraft)—Massachusetts—Salem. 2. Salem
(Mass.)—History.] I. Title.
KFM2478.8 w5z45   1989
345.744.50288—dc19
[347.4405288]
88-38941 CIP AC

to John

Note: Some of the names used in this text have a variety of spellings in reference works. The spellings chosen for use in this book were the most common ones. Other spellings you might encounter are shown below, following the most commonly used spellings:

Sarah Good/Goode
Sarah Osburn/Osburne
Mary Wolcott/Walcott, Wollcott
sabbath/sabbat
Giles Cory/Corey
Elizabeth Howe/How
Susanna Martin/Susannah
Sarah Wildes/Wilds
Proctor/Procter

CONTENTS

THE
SALEM
WITCHCRAFT
TRIALS

A typical "Halloween" witch. Today, we tend to think that all witches look alike, but during colonial times, people believed that witches could take any shape or form.

1

THE DEVIL'S HELPERS

Today, witches depicted in storybooks or on Halloween decorations all look basically alike. They are old, ugly women dressed in black with dirty hair, wrinkled faces, and warts. But people who believed in witches long ago didn't think they all looked the same. They believed that anyone could be a witch.

It may be hard to understand today how so many people in colonial times could have believed in witches, but there were some good reasons for doing so. For one thing, witches were mentioned in the Bible, and more people in the past believed in the Bible literally than do today. For another, religious leaders told the people that witches were doing the Devil's work on earth. Witchcraft was often used to explain frightening natural phenomena, such as illness or storms. In addition, some people actually said that they were witches. A few even bragged about their powers while taking food, clothing, or money from neighbors too frightened to stop them.

In a book entitled *Malleus Maleficarum*, written in 1485, the authors, two clergymen, not only wrote about the history of witches, they also gave their views on why women were more likely than men to become the Devil's helpers. Women, they said, were not as smart as men, and they were greedier. The Devil, then, could easily get a female to work for him by promising to make her rich. The authors also said that because women were jealous of men's superior physical strength, they turned to the Devil for supernatural powers to make themselves strong. Few men could be tricked into working for the Devil, they added, but when they were, it was because women—usually wives—bewitched them and led them astray.

According to the old stories, a witch made a deal with the Devil to do his bidding. To make the agreement official, she signed her name in the Devil's book, and he put his mark on her body. The mark was usually a mole or a scar that was thought to be cold and dead. Once she agreed to the Devil's deal, the witch gathered souls for him by pestering and plaguing good people until they also were willing to sign his book.

People believed that witches also attended meetings on moonlit nights to worship their leader. Called *sabbaths*, the meetings were the opposite of church services. For example, Christians used white bread at communion services; witches were said to use black bread instead. Church members said their prayers for-

In this fifteenth-century woodcut,
the Devil is seen seducing a witch.

A witch gathering

ward; witches were said to mumble them backward. And while church services were quiet and respectful, sabbath services were said to include dancing, with partners back to back, and feasting on garbage and human flesh.

To get to their meetings, witches were said to rub a special lotion all over their bodies that supposedly enabled them to fly. In fact, some suspected witches did make a lotion from herbs and plants. When inhaled, it caused dizziness and strange dreams. It's not surprising that users said they could fly.

Today, historians believe that most of the popular stories about witches and sabbath meetings were made up by people who wanted to convince others that witchcraft existed. Accused witches being tortured to get them to confess often added stories of their own. Beaten for hours or burned with hot irons, they were willing to say anything to end the agony. Other accused witches who were suffering from mental illness added their own deranged fantasies to the tales as well.

In 1484, Catholics, led by Pope Innocent VIII, upset by the increasing number of stories about witchcraft, demanded an end to its practice. All over Europe, hundreds of suspects were rounded up and hanged or burned at the stake.

Witch hunting became a full-time job for a few. Witch hunters traveled from village to village to find the evil ones. Witch hunting paid well. In England, for example, one man who rounded up as many as twenty suspects a day charged villagers twenty shillings for every one he named.

Above: *witches are burned by the Inquisition in a German marketplace.* Below: *the water test was thought to be a way of recognizing a witch.*

Just pointing out a witch wasn't enough, though. Witch hunters had to provide "proof." One form of proof was the "Devil's mark." A suspect was searched, and if any suspicious spot were found, it was tested by jabbing it with a pin. If the accused showed no sign of pain and didn't bleed, it was proof that the mark was dead and clearly the work of the Devil.

Instead of using ordinary pins, some witch hunters had special tools made for sticking suspects. These tools had long handles topped by sharp needles. Later, it was discovered that a few of these handles were hollow, so the needles fixed in them could easily slide backward when pushed against a suspect. Obviously, the accused wouldn't bleed or feel any pain. One witch hunter in England later admitted that he had often used a fake sticker. More than two hundred people were executed because he had "proved" with the fake sticker that they were guilty!

Sometimes a suspect was given a "water test." She was told to bend over, and her hands were tied to her feet, right hand to left foot, left hand to right foot. She was then thrown into a lake or river. If she floated, she was guilty. People believed that the water was so pure, it would not accept a witch but instead would reject her by pushing her body up to the surface. If the accused sank, she was innocent. Many suspects drowned before they could be rescued.

When the Puritans left England to come to the New World in the 1600s, they brought their belief in witches with them (see Chapter Two). Shortly after they arrived, Puritan leaders wrote laws that made witchcraft a crime. Some first offenders were sent out

*The witch hunt in New England
in the early 1690s*

of the colony. This punishment usually meant death because there was no food, shelter, or defense against hostile Indians outside the colony.

Margaret Jones was the first woman to be executed for witchcraft in the American colonies. She was a self-taught doctor and often used mixtures of herbs to cure patients. Her remarkable successes made neighbors suspicious, and they decided she had to be a witch. She was arrested, tried, and hanged in 1648.

Over the next few years, more suspects were arrested. Between 1648 and 1662, at least fourteen witches were hanged. Then, for almost twenty-five years, witchcraft in the New World received little attention.

By the late 1600s, however, the hunt for the Devil's helpers was back on with a vengeance. Puritan ministers were concerned by the growing lack of interest in the church, the loss of church members, and the disrespectful ways that some of the colonists behaved. Since the Puritans believed that one bad person in a colony could bring God's punishment down on all—like a smallpox epidemic—many ministers were worried. They looked for something, such as the common fear of witchcraft, to get the colonists back to the Puritan way of life. Some ministers wrote books about witchcraft to stimulate interest. Others preached about what might happen if the witches among them weren't exposed. They told their flock to watch their neighbors carefully. And watch they did. Shortly thereafter, witches—lots of witches!—began to be spotted in Salem Village, Massachusetts.

2

SOME
BACKGROUND

In the 1500s, Spain had several important colonies in the New World. The Spanish colonists were providing their native land with grain, sugar, exotic fruits, and large quantities of gold and silver. In fact, the colonies were making Spain the wealthiest nation on earth. The English rulers, who wanted a share of the New World's riches, sent explorers to North America to claim land for colonization.

However, the English government couldn't afford to finance settlements on the lands that it eventually claimed, so it encouraged individuals to do it. Sir Walter Raleigh was one of the first men to get involved in such a venture. In 1585, he started a colony on Roanoke Island, which is located off the coast of what is today North Carolina. His colonists suffered from various problems, including a shortage of food. Most returned to England. Raleigh sent more settlers with more food the following year, and for a while it looked as if the colony might become successful. Then Roanoke's leaders went to England to get supplies. When they returned, they found that the rest of the colonists had disappeared. No trace of them was ever found. Raleigh had used up his entire fortune on Roanoke and couldn't finance more settlers. Few others in England were wealthy enough to support a colony; those who were, were afraid to try it after Raleigh's disaster.

However, several years later—again at the encouragement of the English government—merchants, bankers, and investors formed their own companies to finance colonization. These companies sold stock to raise money. Each stockholder would share in the colony's profits according to the number of stocks he or she held.

The London Company started a colony this way in 1607, where Jamestown, Virginia, is today. The colony's beginning was not promising. Settlers expected to find gold, just as the Spanish had in their colonies, and then to move back to England to live in luxury. Because they didn't plan to stay, the settlers refused to build houses, raise crops, or set up a government. It wasn't until Captain John Smith became their leader that the settlement began to thrive. Smith outlawed hunting for gold and ordered everyone to work. Jamestown became the first permanent English settlement in North America. Others were encouraged by its success.

*Sir Walter Raleigh's expedition at Roanoke
Island in 1584 (Raleigh not in picture).*

*The landing at
Jamestown, Virginia*

*Captain John Smith, leader
of the Jamestown settlement*

Another organization, the Plymouth Company, started several colonies in what is now the New England area. The first, located on the Kennebec River, failed. The second, started in 1620 at present-day Plymouth, Massachusetts, was successful. Most of the settlers at Plymouth were religious dissenters. Known as the Pilgrims, they wanted to break away from the Church of England to start their own church. The King of England, who was also the head of the Church of England, vowed to punish them. They avoided this prosecution by fleeing.

A third organization, called the Massachusetts Bay Company, also started several colonies in the New England area. One of these colonies, now known as Salem, Massachusetts, was begun in 1628 by another small group of religious dissenters, the Puritans.

The Puritans wanted to "purify" the Church of England by eliminating many of its elaborate ceremonies and rites, which they thought too closely resembled Catholic masses. They wanted simple services. In the late 1620s the Puritans were threatened with prosecution, just as the Pilgrims had been only a few years before. Puritan leaders looked to New England as a safe place for their followers. By 1630, Puritan leaders had purchased all the stock in the Massachusetts Bay Company. That same year, the company sent nine hundred of its members to the Salem area. By the end of the year, it had sent two thousand settlers to New England. By the middle of the 1640s, the Massachusetts Bay Colony, which included all the Puritan settlements, had fifteen thousand settlers. It was the largest English colony in the New World.

Above: *the landing of the Pilgrims at Plymouth Rock on December 11, 1620. The lithograph is by Sarony & Major.* Below: *the escape of the Puritans to the New World.*

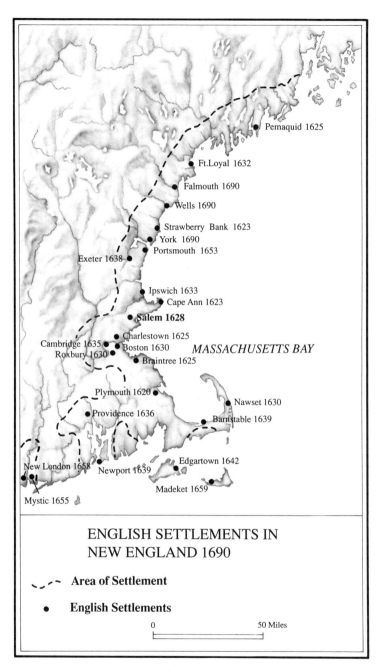

Pemaquid 1625

Ft.Loyal 1632

Falmouth 1690

Wells 1690

Strawberry Bank 1623
York 1690
Portsmouth 1653
Exeter 1638

Ipswich 1633
Cape Ann 1623
Salem 1628

Charlestown 1625
Cambridge 1635
Roxbury 1630
Boston 1630
Braintree 1625

MASSACHUSETTS BAY

Plymouth 1620
Nawset 1630
Providence 1636
Barnstable 1639

New London 1658
Newport 1639
Edgartown 1642
Madeket 1659

Mystic 1655

ENGLISH SETTLEMENTS IN NEW ENGLAND 1690

- - - **Area of Settlement**

● **English Settlements**

0   50 Miles

Nauset 1630

The Massachusetts Bay Company's charter gave the group's leaders, all Puritans, the right to govern the colony. Only male Puritans could vote for government officials. These voters elected "assistants" from a group of men already approved of by the Puritans. The assistants would then choose a governor and members of the legislature. This government would base all the colony's laws on the Bible.

The Massachusetts Bay Company was different from other companies. For one thing, its headquarters was moved from England to Massachusetts. Once it was away from English officials, the company could operate without English interference. Puritan leaders ignored those parts of their charter and any English laws that weakened their control. Also, unlike other companies, the Massachusetts Bay Company's major goal wasn't to make money, especially after the Puritans purchased all of the company's stock. Its main purpose then was to build a perfect religious settlement, one completely free from sin.

Once a government was established, the Puritan leaders concentrated on keeping their settlers faithful. Life was to consist of working hard, praying, going to church, and obeying the colony's strict laws. One's thoughts were always to be on God. Those disagreeing with this way of life—including Quakers, who had quite different ideas from the Puritans—were not welcome. They were threatened with hanging if they stayed.

3

THREE
WITCHES

The first warning that something was wrong in Salem Village, the northwest part of old Salem Town, occurred in January 1692. That was when a strange illness broke out.

Betty Parris was the first to show the symptoms. Overnight, the nine-year-old girl had become very forgetful. She began to spend most of her time—even mealtimes—just staring straight ahead. She also made animal-like noises. These noises, soft and whimpering in the beginning, later turned into loud, frightening sounds, which were followed by bursts of tears.

Abigail Williams, Betty's eleven-year-old cousin who lived with the Parris family, was next. Like Betty, she made strange noises. Unlike Betty, she dropped to her hands and knees and barked like a dog or brayed like a donkey. Sometimes, she would rush about the house with her arms flapping at her sides, as if she were trying to fly.

At first, Reverend Parris and his wife tried to cure the girls themselves. But when both got worse, they sent for the village doctor.

Dr. Griggs gave the girls a complete checkup. When he couldn't find any sign of a recognizable disease, he checked his medical books for clues. But he couldn't find anything in them that might help.

The Parrises took Betty and Abigail to other doctors. All listened to their story, examined the girls carefully, and shook their heads in puzzlement. Like Dr. Griggs, they didn't have any idea what was causing the girls' strange behavior. Shortly after, the mysterious ailment struck two other girls who lived nearby.

Then twelve-year-old Ann Putnam got sick. She, too, made strange sounds. She, too, got down on her hands and knees and crawled around the house on all fours, barking like a dog. But in addition, Ann had terrrible "fits." She fell down and thrashed about, crying for help, screaming in pain. At times her body would stiffen, with her arms and legs frozen and jutting into the air like the limbs of a tree.

During one such fit, Ann's father ran for the doctor. Dr. Griggs checked the girl thoroughly, even though he really didn't expect to find anything that would help him identify the disease. When asked for a reason for Ann's behavior, Griggs told the Putnams what he had lately begun to suspect. In his opinion, Ann and the rest of the afflicted girls were bewitched!

It would have been hard to keep this a secret in a settlement as small as Salem Village. Even though

[32]

the parents of the afflicted girls tried to hide their daughters' illnesses, neighbors found out anyway. Many began to look for an excuse to get a glimpse of the girls. Some even went to their homes to see the fits firsthand. A few thought the girls were acting and needed a good whipping. Most, though, just like the doctor, thought they were bewitched.

One minister visited the Parrises to see for himself what was going on. He saw Abigail rush about trying to fly. He also saw her run to the fireplace, pull out burning pieces of wood, and throw them around the room. The minister agreed with the doctor's diagnosis.

Reverend Parris called for a day of prayer, hoping to find some answers to the girls' problems. Ministers from surrounding towns were asked to come to pray with the local villagers.

The girls were taken to the meetinghouse. At first, all seemed well. The girls behaved normally. But when the prayers started, everything changed. Whenever God's name was mentioned, the girls screamed, as if they were in great pain. As the prayers continued, several fell to the floor in fits. There was so much noise in the room—shouting, moaning, and crying—that the ministers simply couldn't go on. No one now doubted that the girls were bewitched.

It was believed that the victims of witchcraft knew who was hurting them, so the ministers demanded repeatedly that the girls identify their tormentors. They refused.

Reverend Parris wasn't ready to quit, though. He had a suspicion, but he needed to find proof. He knew that his slave, Tituba, had made a "witch cake" from rye flour and the sick girls' urine to try to break their spells. But making such a cake was considered dabbling in witchcraft. If Tituba knew how to break spells, Reverend Parris reasoned, she probably knew how to cast them. Had Tituba actually bewitched the girls and later tried to undo the harm she had done? Or was she simply trying to help the girls by ending another witch's spell?

The reverend questioned Betty again, telling her about the cake. At first, she refused to talk. But when her father kept insisting that she talk, she broke down. Between sobs, she blurted out, "Tituba . . . she . . . oh, Tituba!"[1] then fell into a fit, unable to speak.

What Reverend Parris couldn't learn from Betty, he tried to drag out of Abigail. Then he questioned the rest of the girls, one by one, including Dr. Griggs's niece, who was now also sick.

Eventually, he was able to piece a story together. Betty and Abigail, it seems, had wanted to know what the future held for them. They had often talked about it with Tituba, who had learned about black magic and fortunetelling in her native land, the West Indies. The slave had offered to tell their futures.

Early that winter, the three had gathered in the Parris kitchen for their first session. The slave began by breaking and separating an egg, then dropping the white into a glass of water. This glob served as the group's crystal ball. Tituba gazed into it and said she saw wonderful things.

The girls had enjoyed the fortunetelling so much, they couldn't keep it a secret. They told their friends, who then told their friends. Many wanted to join in

Tituba and the children

the forbidden fun. Soon a number of girls, including Ann Putnam, were visiting the Parris kitchen often to have a peek into their futures.

All went well until one of the girls thought she saw the shape of a coffin in the egg white. Terrified, she begged Tituba to stop. It was the last meeting. Right after that Betty, then the others, got sick.

Reverend Parris was dismayed to learn that such evil activities had taken place in his home. He announced, "Now the Devil hath been raised amongst us."[2] He held Tituba responsible, and he questioned her angrily. At first, Tituba refused to admit to her crimes, but after a thorough beating, she said what he wanted to hear. She admitted that she was a witch and that she had cast spells. She also told Reverend Parris that she was not the only witch. Sarah Good and Sarah Osburn, villagers whom the reverend and others had suspected of witchcraft in the past, had been in league with her.

Eager to end the trouble, Reverend Parris went to the constable. He demanded that the three women be arrested. Warrants were sworn out, and Tituba, Good, and Osburn were arrested and thrown into jail. There they were chained to the wall to make sure they couldn't escape before their hearings were held.

4

THE HEARINGS

Early on the morning of March 1, 1692, the villagers gathered outside the meetinghouse. Each hoped to get a seat at the hearings and to see the arrival of the accused witches and the magistrates, or judges, from Salem Town.

Around noon, two men wearing long black cloaks and high-crowned hats were spotted heading toward the crowd on Meetinghouse Road. Villagers who had been sent down the road earlier that morning to await and greet the magistrates now walked beside or behind them. Some held pennants high in the air. Others beat on drums, setting the pace for the small, solemn parade.

The magistrates, John Hathorne and Jonathan Corwin, were the first to enter the meetinghouse. Once inside, they walked slowly to the front of the room and seated themselves behind a long table brought in for the occasion. In front of them were many rows of long wooden benches, where the spectators would sit.

The seven afflicted girls—Betty, Abigail, Ann, Mercy Lewis (a servant in the Putnam home), Elizabeth Hubbard (Dr. Griggs's niece), plus Susanna Sheldon and Mary Wolcott (neighbors of the Parrises)—came in next. They sat down on the first row of benches, facing the magistrates. Then the rest of the villagers filed in.

When all were seated, the room grew silent. Everyone waited for the suspects to arrive and watched the magistrates arrange papers on the table. These papers contained information about earlier witchcraft trials, and the magistrates had already studied them carefully. They planned to look for three kinds of "proof" that had been used in the past. Even if only one kind could be found, it would be reason enough to hold the suspect for trial.

One kind of "proof" the judges were looking for was the Devil's mark. Each of the accused was to be stripped and searched by a group appointed by the magistrates. Every inch of the suspect's body was to be examined carefully. Every mole, wart, and scar was to be pricked and the result reported at the hearing.

The second kind of "proof" sought was testimony from villagers about past incidents. It was believed at the time that whenever a witch lost an argument, she took revenge by casting a spell. In fact, that was how victims supposedly knew who was hurting them. Therefore, the magistrates planned to ask villagers to recall former troubles. Had anyone's cow died or child gotten sick or crops failed after he or she had had a fight with one of the accused? If the answer was yes, it would be proof of witchcraft.

The third kind of "proof" the judges were looking for was called *spectral evidence*. Spectral evidence was testimony from victims that a suspect's ghostlike spirit—or, as it came to be called, "shape"—had hurt them. The Puritans believed that clever witches could send their spirits or shapes to do their work for them.

Spectral evidence often made for emotional and dramatic presentations by witnesses.

That way, they didn't even have to leave home physically to pester the innocent. This meant that no alibi offered by the accused could be taken into consideration. A witch could even be sitting in the meetinghouse for all to see while her shape was out tormenting someone.

At last, there was a noise outside. Everyone in the room turned and looked toward the door. The accused had arrived!

Goodwife Good—Goody Good for short—was brought in first. Two constables dragged her in, each holding tightly to one of her arms. They had good reason to believe she might try to escape. She had fought with the jailer that morning when he had tried to take her from her cell. Later, on the trip from the jail to the meetinghouse, she had jumped from the horse she was riding and had almost gotten away.

Good's appearance was not what the Puritans expected a woman to look like. Her clothes were tattered, her face was dirty, and her long hair was uncombed and full of snarls.

Her attitude wasn't exactly what they expected, either. She looked around at the audience, matching stare for stare, and laughed as the constables pulled her toward the long table.

Magistrate Hathorne arose. In a voice loud enough for all to hear, he asked, "Sarah Good, what evil spirit have you familiarity with?"

Good answered in a voice almost as loud as Hathorne's, "None."

"Have you made no contract with the Devil?"

"No."

"Why do you hurt these children?"

"I do not hurt them. I scorn it. . . . I am falsely accused."[1]

Unfortunately for Goody Good, she then turned to look at the girls. They fell into fits. Since it was believed that a witch could cast a spell just by looking at a victim, most in the room were now certain Good was a witch.

Hathorne shouted at the woman, "Sarah Good, do you not see now what you have done? Why do you not tell us the truth? Why do you thus torment the children?"

"I do not torment them. . . . It was Osburn."[2]

Hathorne would not accept her claim of innocence. He wanted a confession. He then took testimony from villagers. Many were eager to tell stories about the unpopular beggar woman. Several said she had threatened them when they wouldn't give her money. One man said seventeen of his cows had died shortly after he refused her. This didn't produce a confession from Good, but it was enough proof for the magistrates to decide she should remain in jail.

As Goody Good was taken out, Sarah Osburn was brought in. She, too, was led by the constables. Unlike Good, though, she was too scared and too weak to walk by herself. The sixty-year-old woman had been seriously ill for several months.

Hathorne asked her many of the same questions he had asked Good. Like Good, Osburn denied she was a witch. In fact, she thought that she herself was bewitched and told strange tales about seeing the shape of a tall, dark man who pinched her and hurt her. Her illness, she said, was probably the result of a witch's spell.

Good's testimony, however, that Osburn was a witch was proof enough for Hathorne, even if all three forms of evidence that he and Corwin had decided to look for could not be found. He ordered her returned to jail, too.

Osburn was led out, and Tituba—greeted by the girls' screams and cries—was brought in. As soon as Tituba began to confess, though, everyone was quiet. Her story was so fascinating that no one wanted to miss a word of it.

While Magistrate Corwin took notes, Hathorne questioned the suspect. "Did you ever see the Devil?"

Tituba nodded. "The Devil came to me and bid me serve him."

"Why do you hurt the children?"

"I do not hurt them."

"Who is it then?"

"Four women sometimes hurt the children."

"Who were they?"

"Goody Osburn and Sarah Good, and I do not know who the others were."

"But did you not hurt them?"

"Yes, but I will hurt them no more."

"Why did you hurt them?"

"They [Good and Osburn] say hurt the children or we will do worse to you. . . . I was afraid they would cut off my head."[3]

As Tituba continued, it was clear she had had many interesting visions. She talked about bright yellow birds, red rats, and a strange animal that was sometimes a hog and sometimes a big dog. And, she added, she had actually seen Osburn's "familiar"—an animal that supposedly helps a witch to do her work. Osburn's familiar, she said, was a big yellow dog with a woman's head and wings.

She also admitted that she had gone with Good and Osburn to a witches' sabbath and to Putnam's to hurt Ann. She said she hadn't wanted to go and excused herself for having gone by saying, "They are very strong and pull me, and make me go with them."

"How did you go?"

"We ride upon sticks."[4]

She also told a story about a visit from a tall man. She couldn't see the man's face clearly, but she did see the book he was carrying. When he opened it for her to sign, she saw nine names in it.

Villagers gasped at the news. That meant there were more witches loose in the area!

When Tituba was finally finished confessing—it took three days for her to tell her whole story—she was taken back to jail. There she was chained again in the same cell as Good and Osburn. Their conversations must have been interesting, to say the least!

5

MORE ARRESTS
AND
SOME HANGINGS

Even though Good, Osburn, and Tituba were in jail, the girls' fits didn't go away. Rather, they worsened. Shapes appeared regularly, pinching and choking them. As a result, more arrests were made in March and April 1692, whenever the girls could identify—or in the words the Puritans used, "cry out on"—a tormentor. And although the girls lost Betty when the Parrises sent her away to recover, the group grew. Others joined them, including a young boy.

At first, the new suspects were, like Good and Osburn, old women who were not very well liked. A few, like Good's five-year-old daughter, were confessed witches. Soon, however, some of the most respected people in the area were accused.

One such woman was Rebecca Nurse. Seventy-one years old, Goody Nurse was a faithful church

Arrest of an accused witch

member, a loving wife, a devoted mother, a doting grandmother, and a good neighbor. How, many asked themselves after her arrest, could such a woman be a witch? What proof was there?

Abigail Williams had "proof." She said she had seen Nurse's shape, and it had tormented her in the Parris home. Deodat Lawson, a former village minister, and Reverend Parris had witnessed the tormenting.

It began one night when Abigail screamed that a shape had entered the house. Neither Parris nor Lawson saw anything, no matter how hard they looked. Abigail then pointed toward the middle of the room and shouted in disbelief, "Do you not see her? Why there she stands!"

Then Abigail pushed something away, something she alone saw. "I won't! I won't! I am sure it is none of God's book!"[1]

Lawson demanded that she tell him who she saw. Abigail shouted that she saw Goody Nurse. Then she ran to the fireplace and tried to fly up the chimney to get away from Nurse's shape.

Goody Nurse was arrested. On March 24, she was taken to the meetinghouse for her hearing. The elderly woman's quiet and humble manner touched almost everyone in the room. Her friends wept as she walked toward the magistrates. Hathorne, also affected by her appearance, asked softly for her plea. With quiet confidence, she said that she was innocent.

The girls' reaction to that news was fits. They fell to the floor, some crying and shrieking, others seemingly unable to speak. Witnesses watched their bodies stiffen into grotesque shapes and huge lumps rise in some of their throats. Few doubted they were being bewitched by Nurse.

"Oh, Lord, help me!" Rebecca pleaded.[2]

Now the girls, recovered, began to imitate Nurse's every move. If she turned her head, they turned theirs; if she shifted her feet, they shifted theirs.

Then Ann Putnam's mother joined the girls in accusing Nurse. She told the magistrates that she had seen the ghosts of several village children, who had died years ago, in her dreams. They had told her that Goody Nurse had murdered them, bewitched them to death.

That was enough for the judges. Nurse was taken back to jail to await her trial. Shortly after that, Rebecca's two sisters, who bravely spoke out in her defense, were also arrested and thrown into jail.

In April, Mary Warren was jailed. This arrest was surprising because Warren had been one of the afflicted girls. However, when the other girls cried out on the Proctors, the people Mary worked for and lived with, Mary said they must be lying. Soon after, some of the girls said they thought they saw Mary's shape. On April 19, Mary was asked to explain herself at a hearing.

At first, she seemed strong and sure. But when the girls had fits, her body began to twitch, and she had trouble speaking. She tried, though. "I will speak. Oh, I am sorry for it! I am sorry for it! . . . I will tell! I will tell!" Then she fell into a fit.

When she recovered, she tried to continue. "I will tell! They did . . . they did . . . they did . . ."[3] Then her fit returned, and her jaws locked. She spoke no more that day.

Several days later, she claimed she had been bewitched when she said the girls had lied. She joined in on crying out against the Proctors and took her old place with Ann and the others. They seemed happy to have her back.

The arrests continued. No trials could be held, however, because the colony's charter, which had given local officials temporary power to run the government, had expired. The old charter had been changed several times since it had first been issued in the early 1600s because many colonists had complained to the King of England about the overly strict Puritan laws. For example, the king now appointed the governor rather than allowing the Puritan assistants to elect him. The colony's leader, Increase Mather, had gone to England to get a new charter.

In late May, Increase Mather returned to the colony with a new charter that appointed Sir William Phips, who also went to England, as the new governor. Upon learning that the jails were full of witches, Phips declared that the trials should begin at once. He set up a special court to hear the witchcraft cases, called the Court of Oyer (to hear) and Terminer (to decide).

Phips was planning to leave the colony for an expedition to Canada, so he put Deputy Governor William Stoughton in charge of the court. Stoughton, with help from six experienced judges, was to organize and run the trials. He decided that a jury of twelve male church members should be selected to hear the evidence and decide if the suspects were innocent or not, even though *any* male owning enough property could now be a juror under the new charter. The judges would determine punishment for anyone found guilty. Lawyers would not be allowed to advise suspects, even though the charter did allow this. In fact, lawyers had been forbidden by the Puritans to practice in the colony at all, since it was felt they couldn't be trusted. Stoughton decided to follow that practice. The trials would be held in the courthouse in Salem Town. Meanwhile, magistrates Hathorne and Corwin were expected to continue their hearings for suspects in Salem Village.

The first trial, Bridget Bishop's, was held on June 2. It's not recorded why Bridget was chosen over the others who had been arrested before her, but she and her husband owned two taverns in the area, where laughter and noise continued late into the night. Neighbors had been complaining for years that Bridget was setting a poor example for young people. She even allowed customers to play wild games such as "shovelboard" (shuffleboard) at her taverns.

To make matters worse, Bridget was a pretty woman who liked to dress up and show off. She wore red vests and brightly colored dresses trimmed with lace and lots of ribbons. Her garments were quite a contrast to the simple, gray clothing most Puritans thought proper.

Bishop was accused by five of the girls and twenty-three townspeople, many of whom had long memories. Men testified that they had seen her shape in their dreams, and that Bishop had pinched and hurt them.

*The witch trials in Salem continue;
lithograph by George H. Walker.*

One said he had seen her shape fourteen years before near his child. Shortly after, the baby had died. A confessed witch said that she had seen Bridget at a witches' sabbath. Two men testified that they had found puppets hidden in the cellar wall of her old house when they had torn it down twelve years before. The puppets had had pins stuck in them, something witches did to cast spells.

The jury found the proof of witchcraft over-whelming and pronounced her guilty. The judges sentenced her to death. On June 10, the constable took Goody Bishop from her jail cell to Gallows Hill outside Salem Village. There she was hanged by a long rope dangling from a sturdy branch of a large oak tree.

After Bishop's death, one of the judges resigned. He was disturbed by the kind of evidence that had been accepted at her trial. He questioned whether stories about shapes were really proof, and he refused to listen to any more spectral evidence in the courtroom.

His replacement and the other judges were upset by the resignation. Before holding any more trials, they called on ministers and judges outside the village for advice. Most, including the leading Puritan ministers of the day, warned the men not to accept spectral evidence. Stoughton and the others listened, but they refused to change their minds about stories of shapes as proof and continued to admit spectral evidence.

The judges also asked about using the "touch test." They knew that such a test had been used in English courts to prove charges of witchcraft. The test was based on the idea that the spells a witch cast through her eyes would be turned back if the victim

The hanging of Bridget Bishop

touched the witch. The witch's own evil energy would flow out through the victim's fingertips back into the witch. Such a test was easy to give and easy to judge. The accused was blindfolded, so no more spells could be cast. Then the victim was carried to the witch to touch her. If the fit ended, the accused was found guilty.

Most of those consulted were against the test. They reminded the men that English courts no longer used it. Nevertheless, the Salem judges decided they would have victims touch suspects.

Trials began again at the end of June. Sarah Good, Rebecca Nurse, Sarah Wildes, Elizabeth Howe, and Susanna Martin were accused by a number of the girls and, in some cases, by as many as twenty villagers.

On the other hand, a few villagers showed great courage by testifying for some of the women. Some even signed petitions saying that they believed the women to be good people, not witches. Thirty-nine signed such a paper for Rebecca Nurse.

Ignoring most of the petitions, the jury found four of the suspects guilty and Goody Nurse innocent. All the girls fell into fits when Nurse's innocence was announced.

Since the judges thought Nurse was guilty, too, they reminded the jury members that a witch's mark had been found and that a confessed witch had seen her at a sabbath. The judges then ordered the jury to leave the room and reconsider Nurse's innocence. When the jury members returned, they announced that Goody Nurse was a witch.

On July 19, the five women were taken from their cells, loaded into a cart, and driven up the steep, rocky road to Gallows Hill. Many villagers watched them go by. A few followed them up the hill.

While Rebecca Nurse prayed by the tall oak tree, a minister told Sarah Good to confess. After all, he said, she knew she was a witch. Goody Good, spunky to the end, snarled, "You are a liar. I am no more a witch than you are a wizard [male witch], and if you take away my life, God will give you blood to drink."[4]

Then each woman was made to climb a different ladder. Nooses were slipped over their heads and tightened around their necks. The ladders were pulled away. The five strangled to death. Later, their bodies were cut down and thrown into a shallow grave. Executed witches were not allowed a decent burial.

6

WIZARDS AMONGST US!

At the next trials, held in August, men as well as women were charged with doing the Devil's work. One of the suspects, George Burroughs, had been a minister in Salem Village ten years before. Although Reverend Burroughs hadn't been in the area for years, his shape apparently had. It had choked Ann Putnam.

Ann had also been visited by the ghosts of Burroughs's first and second wives. They told her Burroughs had murdered them, and Ann told others. That didn't surprise some villagers, who had suspected him of evil deeds while he had been hiding behind his disguise as a minister. An arrest warrant was sworn out and a constable went to Maine, where Burroughs was then living, to bring him back for a hearing.

At his hearing, twenty-one villagers spoke out against him. Many witnesses said he had shown supernatural strength. Some said he could stick two fingers into the holes of the cover of a big barrel of molasses and then flip the barrel over and hold it high above his head with little effort. A confessed witch said she had seen him lead a sabbath. One of the girls, Mercy Lewis, a former servant at Burroughs's home but now living with the Putnams, recalled seeing a strange book in his library. It matched the description of the Devil's book that other shapes had been seen carrying. Such evidence was more than enough to have him held for a trial.

At his trial, some of the girls' fits were so severe, they had to be taken from the room. One of the remaining girls accused his shape of biting her. She pointed to teeth marks on her arm. Reverend Burroughs's mouth was pried open, and the judges and jury members compared the shape of his teeth to the marks on the girl's arm. In their opinion, it was a perfect match.

Burroughs added the final blow when he tried to defend himself by saying there was no such thing as a witch or a wizard. Jury members knew better. Several confessed witches were in jail, and six more had already been buried in shallow graves on Gallows Hill. At the very least, Burroughs was a liar! They decided he was a wizard as well.

John Proctor also now found himself in trouble and labeled a wizard for questioning the girls' word back in the spring of 1692, when the hearings had begun. He had even forbidden his servant, Mary Warren, who supposedly had become bewitched, to testify because he thought the girls were playacting. He an-

Reverend George Burroughs is accused of wizardry and is later hung on Gallows Hill.

nounced that if it were left up to the girls, "we should all be devils and witches. They should be had to the whipping post!"[1]

Proctor couldn't prevent Mary from testifying. But when he broke into the courtroom to take her home, he got the girls' attention. That was when some of them started to see his shape and say it was tormenting them.

At first, Mary defended Proctor. But when the other girls cried out on her, she changed her story and accused him, too.

At his trial, John's shape was "spotted" sitting on a judge's lap and next to a dog lying under the judge's table. As his shape supposedly moved around the room, the girls kept track of where it went, and spectators jabbed at it as it passed them by. Clearly he, too, was a wizard.

Proctor's crime had been speaking out against the girls. Assistant Constable John Willard's sin was refusing to arrest suspects. He had helped to bring in some of the first so-called witches, but after they were hanged, he wouldn't arrest any more. The girls cried out on him. Willard tried to escape, which only added to the "proof" piling up against him.

Villagers now came forth with tales of ghosts appearing to them at night, claiming that Willard had murdered them by casting spells. When all the accounts were totaled up, he was accused of having been responsible for at least a dozen deaths. He was sentenced to hang.

George Jacobs was also accused of being a wizard. He was cried out on by six of the girls, including his servant, the "bewitched" Sarah Churchill, and the group's only boy, John Doritch. The confession of Jacobs's granddaughter added the finishing touches. After she was arrested for witchcraft, she confessed that both she and her grandfather had cast spells. Later, she took her statement back, saying she had been tricked into confessing. Her confession had been, she said, "altogether false and untrue . . . which I did to save my life."[2] (So far, no *confessed* witches had been hanged, and no one missed that fact.)

A painting called "The Trial of George Jacobs," by T. H. Matteson

*Convicted witches and wizards
on their way to Gallows Hill*

Even though her statement was read in court, the jury wasn't persuaded that Jacobs was innocent. The judges did show some mercy, though, when they allowed the granddaughter to visit the convicted wizard in jail to ask for his forgiveness.

On August 19, the four convicted wizards and one convicted witch, Martha Carrier, were taken to Gallows Hill. A large crowd followed the prisoners' cart to the tall tree. As a noose was slipped over Reverend Burroughs's head, he began to say the Lord's Prayer. Since it was supposedly impossible for a witch or wizard to say it, spectators were at first stunned. Then a few began to move toward his ladder, and someone shouted "Save him!" More moved forward. Burroughs might have escaped the noose if a minister present hadn't stopped them. He demanded their attention and told them that the Devil was playing a trick. He insisted that Burroughs was not what he appeared to be. The hangings went on as planned.

7

THE CORYS

Sometimes witchcraft seemed to run in families. The Carrier, Jacobs, Proctor, Good, Hobbs, Nurse, and Cory families all had more than one member accused of witchcraft. In the Cory family, both Martha and her husband Giles were accused.

Martha was a strong-willed woman who didn't believe in witchcraft. However, her husband Giles did. When the first hearings were held in April, he wanted to attend them. Martha asked him not to and hid his saddle, hoping that would stop him. Giles, just as stubborn as Martha, rode his horse bareback to the meetinghouse.

Ann Putnam said she had seen Goody Cory's shape for the first time right after Martha hid the saddle. Several villagers went to visit Goody Cory to find out if she was practicing witchcraft. When Martha was told that Ann Putnam had seen her shape, she asked if Ann had described what her shape had worn. Ann hadn't been able to describe Martha's clothing, claiming her shape was so bright it had blinded her. When the villagers couldn't answer Martha's question, she laughed in triumph.

This question was not a laughing matter to the villagers, however. How did Martha know that Ann had been questioned about the shape's clothing if Martha hadn't attended the hearings? Goody Cory told them that her husband had told her all about the hearings. But Giles denied this, and Martha was in serious trouble.

Giles didn't help matters any at her hearing when he admitted that there could be a reason or two to believe Martha practiced witchcraft. He testified that he found it difficult to pray when she was around. Furthermore, he added, she often sent him to bed early so she could pray without being overheard. He thought she was trying to hide something.

Martha added to her own troubles at her trial. Because she didn't take the accusations seriously, she didn't always answer the judges' questions directly. For example, when several of the girls claimed they saw a man's shape whispering in Goody Cory's ear in the courtroom, one judge turned to Martha and asked her to tell what the man had said. Martha should have denied that anyone was whispering in her ear right away. Instead, she replied, "We must not believe all that these distracted children say."[1] The judges and jury took that answer to be the words whispered in her ear.

Martha Cory defies her accusers.

As they had done at other trials, the girls followed the accused's every move. They bit their lips when Cory bit hers, crying out in pain as they did so. Some villagers in the audience also said they were affected by Martha's moves. When Martha leaned sharply over a chair, for example, one woman felt a sudden, sharp pain in her stomach. Enraged at Cory for hurting her, she took off one of her shoes and threw it, hitting the so-called witch on the side of the head.

Goody Cory had been charged with witchcraft several years before this. At that time, the charges couldn't be proven. This time, it was different. Cory was found guilty and sentenced to hang.

Goodman Cory was arrested because Ann Putnam had seen his shape. She said that it didn't torment her as others had, though. Instead, it confessed to murder by witchcraft. Giles's shape bragged that Giles had killed his first wife. It said he wanted to kill Martha, too, but since she was a witch, this was a tricky thing to do.

Several villagers testified at Giles's hearing. They had seen a witches' sabbath from their windows late one night. At least fifty witches had been drinking blood-red wine and gobbling down black bread. The villagers didn't recognize all present, but they did get a good look at Giles's face. They ended their testimony by saying that they believed Giles was a wizard. Others nodded in agreement.

Giles was brought in to enter his plea, but he refused to speak. Since a prisoner had to plead "guilty" or "innocent" before a trial could be held, the judges ordered him to talk. When he wouldn't, they ordered him tortured until he was willing to plead.

Giles, who was eighty years old, was taken to a nearby field where the constables made him lie down on his back. A long, wide board was placed on top of him, and big rocks were placed on top of that, one after another. Now and then, the constables asked for a plea. Giles asked for more weight. Eventually, his bones broke and his lungs collapsed. Giles died a slow, painful death.

Goodman Cory probably didn't plead guilty because he knew he was already doomed. In addition, he may not have wanted to give the girls the satisfaction of seeing him hanged. And since no trial could be held,

The trial of Giles Corey

the Cory property could not be seized by the constables, as the property of many others scheduled for trial had been. His children could at least have that much to ease the pain and shame of having parents accused of witchcraft!

More than one villager wondered afterward whether justice had been done in this case. But at least one, Ann Putnam, thought it had. Ann, who saw more shapes and ghosts than most, said she had been visited by yet another ghost. This one told of being pressed to death years ago by Giles. It also said that the pressing of Giles was the right thing to do since, "It must be done to him as it was done to me."[2]

The continued hangings and Giles Cory's death frightened the accused witches in jail. They knew there was little hope for them. Some of them asked for lawyers, but since lawyers weren't allowed, one of the accused witches, Mary Easty (Rebecca Nurse's sister), wrote a letter asking the judges to help them. Goody Easty had already been convicted and was scheduled to die. She made it clear in her letter that she wasn't asking help for herself. But since she knew she was not guilty, she believed that there must be others who were innocent, too. She feared many more innocent people would hang unless something were done.

Goody Easty questioned the proof used at trials, especially confessed witches' statements. Their testimony, she said, was false. They gave it only to save their own lives, knowing they could stay alive only by crying out on others.

The judges were not persuaded, and they refused to change the kinds of proofs that could be given in court. They thought they were clearing the land of witches, and they weren't going to change their ways now.

On September 22, eight more women, including Martha Cory and Goody Easty, were hanged. This time, there was much sadness among the spectators. More and more, the villagers were beginning to feel that something was terribly wrong, that maybe, just maybe, the villagers hanging from the tree weren't really the Devil's helpers after all.

8

NEW YEAR,
NEW RULES

The Salem Villagers who were wondering whether justice was being done weren't alone. The strongest objections to what was happening, however, came from people outside the village. Many colonial ministers—Puritan and otherwise—had already warned the Salem judges about accepting shapes as proof. When the trials continued in the same old way, as did the hangings, they objected again. One even published a booklet attacking spectral evidence.

Citizens in nearby Andover spoke out, too. They were alarmed when the witch hunt seemed about to spread to their town. Ann Putnam and Mary Wolcott had been invited there by one of Andover's ministers to find witches and wizards.

At first, the girls were taken from house to house to see if they could spot any shapes. Then, to save time, suspects were rounded up and brought to the girls. Ann and Mary identified more than forty Devil's helpers in two days, mostly through the touch test.

The accused were about to be arrested. However, after signing the first forty warrants, a local magistrate refused to sign any more. He wondered aloud how so many witches could live in one small town.

Some citizens took action. They signed petitions calling the girls "distempered" (mentally ill). One of the suspects started a lawsuit against the girls for ruining his good name. Suddenly, the hunt ended in Andover.

The colony's leader, Governor Phips, joined the growing number of doubters when he returned from his long expedition to Canada. He was shocked to find over one hundred and fifty suspects in jail, some of them children. He was even more shocked to learn that people had been hanged on spectral evidence alone. And he was astounded to discover that his wife was now among the accused.

Since the warrants had been legally issued, Phips couldn't just turn the suspects loose. He could, however, try to help the accused and see that justice was done. He stopped the trials in October and wrote to leaders in England for advice.

Even before he received their replies, he took action. First, he released most of the accused, especially the children, from jail. He argued that with winter coming, too many might become ill in the unheated cells. He promised that trials would still be held, but the suspects could go home until then. Secondly, he dismissed the Court of Oyer and Terminer. Courts in surrounding towns would be used instead. This meant that jurors who did not know either the accused or the accusers would hear the evidence. Furthermore, from now on, *any* males who owned enough property—not just church members—would be jurors, just as the charter Phips brought back from England in May 1692 said they could.

On January 3, 1693, the first trials were held under the new rules. Fifty-two suspects were brought in, and forty-nine of them were quickly released. Without stories about shapes, which had been disallowed, there was no evidence against most of them. Three women, described by some villagers as "senseless," were found guilty. Governor Phips pardoned them later. Other trials went much the same way until most of the charges of witchcraft were dropped.

When accused witches started bringing lawsuits against their accusers, as the man in Andover did, villagers stopped crying out on other villagers. And then—quite suddenly, in fact—the girls' fits disappeared.

9

QUESTIONS
AND ANSWERS

Had those hanged on Gallows Hill gotten a fair trial? villagers began to wonder. Many also wondered—some for the first time—if the girls had really been bewitched. But if not, why had they acted the way they did?

Some villagers insisted that the girls had been under a spell. If they hadn't been bewitched by the accused, well then, they had been bewitched by the Devil himself.

Others argued that the girls had only been pretending to be under a spell. They said that Abigail Williams and the others had just wanted attention, and acting as if they were bewitched had certainly gotten them that. When they saw that they were believed, they suddenly found that they had power to make things happen as well, and power is hard to give up. That was why the crying out continued.

There is some evidence that the girls were pretending. For example, one night, when several villagers and afflicted girls were together, one of the girls claimed that she saw Goody Proctor's shape. However, when the villagers challenged her claim, she just shrugged her shoulders. She didn't show fear, and she didn't fall to the floor in a fit.

On another occasion, several girls were taken to a nearby town to find witches. They had fits when a group of strangers approached them on the road. But when none of the strangers reacted to them, the girls just got up and went on their way.

In addition, two girls tried to confess. Even though Mary Warren never finished her testimony, her words "I am sorry for it" and "I will tell, I will tell" indicated that she had something urgent to say. A month later, another girl said the afflicted girls were lying. But when both Mary and the other girl were accused of witchcraft, they took their confessions back. They claimed they had been bewitched when they called the girls liars—and probably saved their own lives.

In addition, one of the girls lied at Goody Good's trial. She claimed Good's shape had attacked her with a knife. Spectators gasped when the girl held up the weapon, a part of a knife blade. However, a man in the audience claimed that the blade was his, not Good's. He said he had broken it while carving on a piece of wood before the trial began. He also said that the girl had seen him do it. Then he held up his knife handle with its remaining piece of blade. The edge of his broken blade and the girl's matched!

However, historians who have studied the old Salem trial records do not think the girls were pretending to be bewitched. At least, not all of them were pretending all the time. They point out that the girls rolled about on the floor with such force during a fit that two men couldn't hold one girl down. Historians think the girls were suffering from hysteria.

Typically, hysterics have strong emotional outbursts—crying and screaming—that are followed by unusual physical ailments or bizarre actions. For instance, doctors studying the illness have noticed that

Historians think that some of the afflicted girls may have suffered from hysteria.

hysterics may lose their voice or sight or become paralyzed for no detectable physical reason. Some have violent fits. Huge lumps rise in their throats, and victims complain that they are being choked. Sometimes their bodies stiffen. At other times they may injure themselves by pulling out their hair or throwing themselves against furniture or walls. And sometimes, hysterics make unusual animal-like noises. When the outbursts and fits end, hysterics appear to be completely normal.

Hysterics have uncanny physical and mental powers. They can actually cause rashes or marks to appear on their bodies by believing—really believing—they have rashes or marks. With a few suggestions, hysterics can be made to "see" and "hear" things no one else does. In addition, many hysterics, when they see that their fits get them attention, learn how to bring on a fit whenever they want to.

Doctors believe that a deep-seated, perhaps unconscious fear of something is often the cause of an attack of hysteria. Many normal people experience a mild form of hysteria when they have had a scare. For example, a person may experience a big lump in his or her throat just before giving a speech or taking a test. The fear of failure or embarrassment makes that person feel physically uncomfortable. A normal person faces his or her fears, but an hysteric runs away from problems by becoming ill. Often, when an hysteric is part of a close-knit group, when one person becomes sick from fear, so do the rest. When the illness spreads to others, it is called *mass hysteria*.

There have been several studies of incidents of

mass hysteria. One outbreak took place in England in the late 1700s. It started when a girl slipped a mouse inside her friend's blouse at work. The friend, who was terrified of mice, became hysterical. Her fits were violent and lasted for a whole day.

The next day, three of her friends at work—who hadn't seen the mouse but saw the fit—became ill. The following day, six more fell ill. Eventually, the hysteria spread to twenty-four workers. Many feared that what they had seen was the result of some strange disease. When workers found out that a mouse had caused the first fit, the hysteria stopped.

Historians point out that the Salem girls' behavior matches the general description of hysteria. The girls' fits were certainly similar to hysterics' fits. Many of the girls complained about marks and bruises on their bodies that they believed shapes had given them, shapes no one else saw. More than one enjoyed the attention she was getting and seemed to be able to bring on a fit whenever she wanted. The girls had good reason to be afraid if they really believed that their fortune-telling had raised the Devil. And finally, the girls who became ill were all close friends.

Whether or not the girls were pretending or hysterical, villagers were quite willing to believe their stories. Why?

First, historians think that many of the villagers believed they had seen shapes themselves. Quite a few testified to that in court. It's quite likely that what they thought they saw was the result of their active imaginations or the effects of the powerful herbs often used to cure illness then. Leaves from many different plants—even weeds—were gathered and brewed in hot water to be given as medicine. Many were safe, and some made the patient better. But if the medicines weren't prepared just right or the patient took too much of a liquid, dizziness, bad dreams, or even hallucinations could occur. Anyone could "see" shapes then, especially if he or she believed in them.

Second, the villagers may have supported the girls because they knew that this was not the first time children had "uncovered" a hotbed of witches. English records used as guides in the Salem trials mentioned earlier cases. In one instance, twenty women were killed because a young boy cried out on them.

Third, villagers were influenced by testimony given in court. Several suspects said they were witches. There is some evidence that a few of the suspects— Tituba and possibly George Burroughs—really did try to cast spells. Some villagers may have known that for a fact.

Two modern-day historians, Paul Boyer and Steven Nissenbaum, weren't content with these reasons, however. They thought there might be other reasons why the villagers were so willing to accept the girls' accusations, and they set out to find them. They wondered if the accused had something in common, something that made them different from other villagers and likely suspects. The two historians made a list of all of the accused. They located copies of old records, including birth certificates, so they could figure out the ages of the suspects when the trials began; tax receipts to determine their wealth; and church membership lists to see if the suspects belonged to the local church. When the research was done, the two historians hadn't found anything significant that the suspects had in common. The list of accused included old and young, rich and poor, men and women, and some who were church members and some who were not.

Unwilling to give up, Boyer and Nissenbaum continued their research. They found an old map of the village that another historian, Charles Upham, had drawn of the village when he was studying the trial records in the 1860s. Upham's map was based on old property deeds. He had also visited Salem to measure off plots of land to make sure his map was as accurate as possible. When finished, it showed where almost everyone had lived in the village in 1692. When Boyer and Nissenbaum examined the map, they noticed that almost all the accused lived on the east side of the village, and almost all the accusers, including the girls, lived on the west side.

The two historians then tried to find out what had split the village into two groups. After examining more old records, they discovered that most of the villagers living on the east side, many of them merchants like Proctor and Bishop, had become prosperous over the years. Villagers living on the west side, however, were mostly farmers and were experiencing hard times. The farmers felt they were being taxed unfairly—the historians found copies of some of their petitions—and complained bitterly as their incomes went down year after year. Boyer and Nissenbaum also learned that the two groups had quarreled for more than twenty years about the village's ministers. The three ministers before Reverend Parris had slowly been driven out of

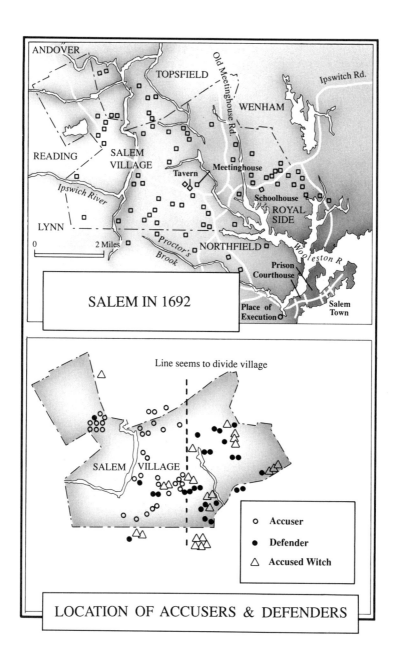

SALEM IN 1692

Line seems to divide village

SALEM VILLAGE

○   Accuser

●   Defender

△   Accused Witch

LOCATION OF ACCUSERS & DEFENDERS

Salem when one side of the village or the other had refused to pay anything toward the ministers' salaries.

The quarrels over taxes and ministers created great anger and many enemies in the village. Boyer and Nissenbaum believe that the girls' accusations were accepted by so many villagers because they were directed against longtime enemies. Many friends of the accused were afraid to defend the suspects, fearing they would be attacked or accused if they said anything.

There is proof that the fight over the ministers affected the witch hunts. One of the families involved in a quarrel over a minister was the Putnam family. Goody Putnam's sister had married the village's first minister. Putnam's sister was in poor health, and her husband's struggle to collect his wages and keep his job didn't help matters any. When her sister died, Goody Putnam blamed the villagers, who had caused her sister so much grief, for her death. And when the accusations started, Ann named the people her mother thought had been responsible for her sister's death.

For whatever reason or reasons, the girls made accusations and the villagers listened and supported them. The only way the trials could be stopped was through outside interference. But Governor Phips was the only one with enough power to do that, and he was in Canada. And so the hunt lasted for eleven months.

10

AFTERWARD

After the witch hunts stopped, everyone looked around to see what damage had been done. Nineteen people had been hanged. One person had been pressed to death. Two people had died in prison, and several had lost their sanity there. And some were still in prison. Since the property of the accused had often been seized by the constables before the trials had even begun, some suspects had only their lives left. As a result, a few were unable to pay their prison bills, the cost of feeding, sheltering, and chaining them. Although Phips freed many of the suspects until the trials could be held, those who had no money had to remain in jail, their bills getting bigger and bigger until friends or neighbors could help them out.

Tituba was one of those who remained in jail. She was held there for over a year, until a man in Boston who heard about her plight paid her bill. Then he took Tituba to the city as his slave.

It was not only the accused and confessed witches who suffered. There was a real shortage of food in the village in the winter of 1692–93, in part because of the witch hunt. Farmers had been so busy attending hearings and trials that many had failed to take care of their crops. Some farmland taken from suspects wasn't planted or harvested.

The Parrises had additional troubles. Many villagers turned against them and refused to go to church as long as Reverend Parris preached there. Some stopped contributing money toward his salary. Reverend Parris actually sued church members to get his wages. By 1695, the reverend was having so many problems with his congregation, he began to think about leaving Salem Village. When his congregation offered him money to go, he packed his family's belongings and left.

Reports on what eventually happened to most of the afflicted girls are scarce. However, we do know a little about two of them, Abigail Williams and Ann Putnam.

Abigail had been disliked by many in the village even before the trials. She had often been thought of as a troublemaker, and a mean-spirited one. Many blamed her for starting the fortunetelling sessions that led to so much trouble. And afterward quite a few villagers decided that she was nothing more than a liar. Abigail, who had liked the attention she had gotten in 1692, went on to do many more things to shock the villagers. For example, she eventually became a prostitute. This was very embarrassing to all those who had supported her and believed in her during the trials.

Ann Putnam had a hard life. A few years after the trials ended, her parents died. She had to take care of her younger brothers and sisters without much help from anyone. To gain acceptance and forgiveness from the village, Ann finally decided to make a public apology for her part in the witch hunts. The minister read her statement aloud in church. She wrote, "I desire to be humbled before God. . . . It was a great delusion. . . . I did it not out of anger, malice, or ill will."[1]

Many besides Ann tried to make up for what had happened. At least one judge and almost all the jurors made public apologies. After such statements, the courts were more willing to grant the requests of children of executed witches and wizards when they pleaded to have their parents' property returned to them and their names cleared. In some cases, where property couldn't be returned, relatives were given money to cover some of the losses.

Those who didn't have children weren't cleared for over two hundred years, however. In 1950, a distant relative of an executed witch asked a court in Massachusetts to officially pardon and drop all charges against her relative and the rest of the convicted witches. The court refused. The judges said they couldn't do this since the colony had been under English control when the trials took place. Therefore, they argued, an English court had to clear the names. The English courts disagreed. Finally, the Massachusetts state legislature took matters into its own hands and in 1957 cleared the names of all concerned.

Villagers tried to do their part in remembering the dead by setting aside days for fasting and prayer. Colonists outside the village remembered the dead, too, by changing some of the colonies' laws. Witchcraft would no longer be listed as a crime punishable by death in most colonies. Of course, this couldn't right the terrible wrongs that had been committed in Salem Village, but it probably did prevent some future wrongs from happening. And that would have pleased Goody Good and all the rest who were hanged on Gallows Hill.

NOTES

Chapter Three
Three Witches

1. Marion Starky, *The Devil in Massachusetts* (New York: Alfred A. Knopf, 1949), 32.
2. Charles Upham, *Salem Witchcraft*, vol. 1 (Boston: Wiggens and Burt, 1867, reprinted 1971), 95. Upham took this quotation from Reverend Parris's church record book, where the reverend had recorded the events in his home—the fortunetelling and the baking of the "witch cake"—that had made him so upset.

Chapter Four
The Hearings

1. W. Elliot Woodward, *Records of Salem Witchcraft*, vol. 1 (Roxbury: private printing, 1864, reprinted in 1969), 17–18. Hathorne's questions and Sarah Good's answers were recorded by Ezekeill Chevers at the hearing. Woodward assembled all the old handwritten records and had printed copies made of them.
2. Ibid., 18–19.
3. Ibid., 44–45.
4. Ibid., 46–47.

Chapter Five
More Arrests and Some Hangings

1. Starky, *The Devil in Massachusetts*, 56. Starky's account of Abigail's behavior and statements first appeared in Deodat Lawson's "Brief and True Narrative," which the minister wrote after witnessing many strange events in Salem.
2. Ibid., 72.
3. Ibid., 90.
4. Ibid., 176. Sarah Good's answer to the minister was first recorded in a pamphlet called "More Wonders of the Invisible World." It was written by Robert Calef, who witnessed some of the events in Salem, including Good's hanging.

Chapter Six
Wizards Amongst Us!

1. Chadwick Hansen, *Witchcraft at Salem* (New York: George Braziller, 1969), 53.
2. Upham, *Salem Witchcraft*, 316. Upham took these words from a copy of Margaret Jacobs's written confession, which was read in the courtroom.

Chapter Seven
The Corys

1. Starky, *The Devil in Massachusetts*, 60.
2. Ibid., 212. Ann's quotation was taken from a letter that her father wrote that told about the ghost's visit and recorded what the ghost had supposedly said.

Chapter Ten
Afterward

1. Starky, *The Devil in Massachusetts*, 271.

BIBLIOGRAPHY

Alderman, Clifford Lindsey. *A Cauldron of Witches*. New York: Julian Messner, 1971.
————. *The Devil's Shadow*. New York: Julian Messner, 1967.
Aylesworth, Thomas G. *Servants of the Devil*. Reading, Mass: Addison-Wesley, 1970.
Boyer, Paul, and Steven Nissenbaum. *Salem Possessed: The Social Origins of Witchcraft*. Cambridge: Harvard University Press, 1974.
Burr, George Lincoln, ed. *Original Narratives of Early American History: Narratives of the Witchcraft Cases, 1648–1706*. New York: Charles Scribner's Sons, 1914.
Chitwood, Oliver Perry. *A History of Colonial America*. New York: Harper and Brothers, 1948.
Coleman, James C. *Abnormal Psychology and Modern Life*. Chicago: Scott Foresman, 1964.
Davidson, James West, and Mark Hamilton Lytle. *After the Fact: The Art of Historical Detection*. New York: Alfred A. Knopf, 1982.
Drake, Samuel. *Annals of Witchcraft in New England and Elsewhere in the United States*. New York: Benjamin Bloom, 1869, reprinted 1967.
Goldenson, Robert, *Mysteries of the Mind*. New York: Doubleday, 1973.
Hansen, Chadwick. *Witchcraft at Salem*. New York: George Braziller, 1969.

Karlsen, Carol F. *The Devil in the Shape of a Woman: Witchcraft in Colonial New England.* New York: W. W. Norton, 1987.

Menninger, Karl. *The Human Mind.* New York: Alfred A. Knopf, 1957.

Miller, John C., ed. *The Colonial Image.* New York: George Braziller, 1962.

Nevins, W. S. *Witchcraft in Salem Village in 1692.* Salem: Salem Press, 1916.

Starky, Marion. *The Devil in Massachusetts.* New York: Alfred A. Knopf, 1949.

Upham, Charles W. *Salem Witchcraft*, vol. 2. Boston: Wiggens and Burt, 1867, reprinted 1971.

Veith, Ilza. *Hysteria, the History of a Disease.* Chicago: University of Chicago Press, 1965.

Woodward, W. Elliot. *Records of Salem Witchcraft*, vol. 1. Roxbury: private printing, 1864, reprinted 1969.

INDEX

ABOUT THE
AUTHOR

*Karen Zeinert, a graduate of Wisconsin State
University, Eau Claire, with a major in history,
is a former teacher of English, reading, and
U.S. history at the middle school and high school
levels. She has written teaching materials on the
history of Wisconsin for Badger House Publications
and teaching strategies for a history textbook
published by McDougal, Littell. She has also
written numerous articles on a variety of subjects
for adult and juvenile periodicals and a book
on keeping chinchillas as pets.*

*Ms. Zeinert is married to a high school history
teacher, John Zeinert, and her hobbies include
gardening and raising chinchillas. She and her
husband make their home in Neenah, Wisconsin.*